DEFEAT YOUR DEMONS

A Practical Guide to Self-Mastery and Inner Strength

Empower Your Life with Real-World Case Studies & Hands-On Exercises to Defeat Your Inner Demons and Triumph!

RYAN SIBELO

Disclaimer: While the author of this book is a trained coach and instructor and has shared experiences and lessons to educate and guide readers, the content within is not intended to be a substitute for professional medical advice, diagnosis, or treatment. The author does not provide medical advice. If at any point while reading this book you feel the need for professional medical assistance, please seek it from a qualified healthcare provider immediately.

I thank everyone who supported me in writing this book for their faith, inspiration, love and friendship.

Published by Ryan Sibelo

Den Haag, Netherlands

First Edition: July, 2023

ISBN: 978-90-9037611-0

Table of Contents

Preface

THE GENESIS OF "DEFEAT YOUR DEMONS"

From an early age, I was fascinated by the world of martial arts. It was a realm where the mind and body intertwined, moving in harmony to create something potent and compelling. As I delved deeper, training to become one of the highest-level Krav Maga instructors, I discovered a parallel between the discipline I practiced and the trials we face in life. This journey not only taught me about strength, endurance, and technique but unveiled a landscape filled with inner demons, each one a challenge to overcome.

I began to see patterns in my behavior and responses to events around me. Some were beneficial, steering me toward my goals, while others were obstructive, influenced by past traumas and deeply ingrained habits. I realized that these habits, these 'demons,' were echoes of past hurts and fear.

They were the manifestations of the protective mechanisms of our 'ego mind,' mechanisms developed to guard us from pain and trauma but often holding us back from growth and self-realization.

My mission with "Defeat Your Demons" was born from these realizations and the desire to share them. I've spent over a decade coaching adults, children, and businesses worldwide. Now, I aim to help readers confront their own demons, empowering them to seize control over their minds, bodies, and ultimately, their lives.

We all bear the imprints of our past. Between the tender ages of zero and eight, we form survival mechanisms, reactions to the world around us based on our experiences. The traumas inflicted upon us, intentional or unintentional, shape these mechanisms. As we grow, we have the chance to evaluate these learned behaviors and decide whether they serve us or hinder us.

So far, the journey has been rewarding. I've had the privilege to engage with incredibly strong and inspiring individuals and organizations, helping them on their path to self-realization and empowerment. Through Defeat Your Demons, I hope to be a beacon, guiding readers towards self-mastery, and aiding in their journey towards freedom, strength, and happiness.

The essence of "Defeat Your Demons" is this: We are blessed with three incredible gifts at birth - the mind, body, and soul. The journey of life is about learning and mastering these elements to allow our inner light to shine upon the world. It's about transcending our ego, releasing harmful energies, and breaking free from the chains of manipulation and influence.

In sharing this journey, I hope to inspire you to understand yourself better, free yourself from harmful influences, and emerge stronger, more resilient, and capable of forming fulfilling relationships. I believe in a world where everyone can harness their intelligence fully and be physically adept - a world where everyone can truly say, "I have defeated my demons."

Welcome to the journey towards self-mastery. Let's defeat our demons together.

What This Book Can Do For You

This book is not just a collection of words; it's a potent tool, an ally on your journey to empowerment. It is my hope that this book will inspire you and act as a guide towards a life that is natural and intrinsic to us as humans: a life that's "Powerful and Free" — one filled with love for ourselves, others, and the world we inhabit. It is designed to encourage introspection, aiding you in understanding your past and how it influences your present, and empowering you to shape a better future.

Each chapter in this book provides you with exercises, insights, and affirmations that you can apply to your daily life. These are your stepping stones on your journey to defeating your demons. You'll find that as you implement these, you'll be in a better position to replace harmful behaviours and thought patterns with positive ones.

From this book, you can expect a call to action — a call to connect deeply with yourself, to unravel your childhood traumas, and understand the behaviours that sprouted from these traumas. This book encourages you to take the necessary steps, even seeking professional help if necessary, to face and defeat your inner demons. By recognizing and changing harmful survival mechanisms, you will begin to listen more to your intuition, reducing your reliance on external advice.

"Defeat Your Demons" complements the overall ethos of our brand. While this book helps you on a personal level, the Defeat Your Demons clothing line serves as a constant reminder of your journey. Our podcast, featuring successful entrepreneurs and martial artists, will be an inspirational source demonstrating the potential to overcome obstacles and thrive. The YouTube channel will further enrich your experience, providing you with a wealth of related content.

To illustrate the transformative power of the principles in this book, let me share a story of one of my clients. She had been attacked in her youth and had developed a limiting belief about her ability to protect herself, a demon that held her back from living a free and powerful life. Through my coaching and the methodologies outlined in this book, she learned to challenge these limiting beliefs. She learned that defending oneself is not only necessary but also an act of self-love, and it's okay to stand up for yourself, even if it means causing harm to someone who intends to harm you.

I share this story because it's not an isolated case. Many people find themselves trapped by similar limiting beliefs, often implanted during their early years. This book will help you identify and dismantle such beliefs, replacing them with empowering thoughts and behaviours.

In short, "Defeat Your Demons" aims to equip you with the knowledge and tools to break free from the chains of harmful habits and negative beliefs. It will assist you on your journey towards a strong, independent, and joy-filled life. And remember, the universe begins to assist you the moment you commit to becoming your best self. So, are you ready to defeat your demons?

Introduction

THE BATTLEFIELD OF THE MIND AND BODY

In the vast landscape of our existence, our mind and body stand as a battlefield. A battle waged between our intuition and outside influences, between short-term gratifications and long-term goals. This book is a tribute to the resilience of the human spirit in this ongoing struggle, an acknowledgment of our constant endeavor to assert our authentic selves in the face of adversities.

Life has taught me, through my own personal experiences and those of the people I've coached, that we're often entangled in a war against forces, both external and internal, that seek to control, manipulate, or undermine our true essence. Whether it is dependencies on opinions, substances, or even people, these elements aim to shift our focus away from our long-term objectives, and instead, tempt us towards fleeting satisfactions.

The journey towards my first black belt degree in Krav Maga serves as a vivid illustration of this struggle. Over seven strenuous years, I battled numerous distractions and influences that appealed to my immediate gratification but would have ultimately steered me away from my goal. It was the fiery passion and the relentless determination that guided me through, helping me understand the essence of the constant battle between our immediate desires and our ultimate goals.

But it is not just about the physical or external. There is an equally compelling internal dynamic at play. The ego, with its protective shield of emotions, often clashes with our intuition, which remains untouched by feelings like fear, anger, or happiness. This conflict can influence our behavior, and if we aren't mindful, it can steer us away from our inherent brilliance.

As you embark on this journey through these pages, embrace the reality that life is a battlefield. Pain, loss, and suffering are inevitable, much like the skirmishes in a battlefield. But remember, every challenge you face and overcome adds to your credibility, resilience, and knowledge. It is this strength that enables you to shine your light brighter in the world and serve your purpose.

To prepare for this journey, here's an exercise: Recite the following affirmations, "I am a Soldier of Light. Any and every battle I've fought and will fight in this life is here to make me stronger, more skilled, resilient, knowledgeable, and helpful to others." This mantra will serve as your armor, guarding your resolve as you navigate the battlefield of the mind and body.

As we venture further into the exploration of this battlefield, let's pledge to stay vigilant and unwavering. Let's promise to defeat our demons, empowering ourselves and others around us. Remember, the journey may be strenuous, but the rewards are worth every battle.

Chapter 1

THE ECHOES OF CHILDHOOD

Understanding the Impact of Childhood Trauma

Childhood traumas, such as parents divorcing, violence at home, feeling emotionally ignored or neglected, continuous teasing, abuse, or betrayal by someone you trusted, can deeply shape who we become. These experiences can often lead to the development of social or mental coping mechanisms as a means of survival. Our minds are forced to create their own positive environments or learn to express physical or emotional sensations in atypical ways. These coping mechanisms can sometimes manifest as conditions such as personality disorders or attention deficit disorders.

Research has shown that adverse childhood experiences can result in significant mental health and social issues later in life, from depression and anxiety to difficulties in forming healthy relationships.

Case study: Confronting Coping Mechanisms - The Path to Self-Mastery

The Environment: Growing up amid divorce, violence, and emotional neglect, I faced both intended and unintended physical or emotional abuse. This turbulent environment led to the development of Attention Deficit Disorder (ADD) and a pattern of seeking material success for validation.

The Impact and Resulting Behavior:

These coping behaviors helped me avoid stress and pain but had a negative impact. I became focused on "fun" or "happy" things and material possessions, thinking they would make me attractive or liked. They were mechanisms to survive but began to hinder growth in areas like academics, fitness, and relationships.

Overcoming the Challenge:

Realizing these coping strategies were holding me back, I embarked on a journey of self-discovery. Through introspection, I analyzed my behaviors, understanding their origins, and thanking myself for surviving those painful moments. Recognizing they were now impediments, I consciously decided to build healthier strategies.

Transforming Pain into Strength:

By lovingly accepting my past and releasing the old coping mechanisms, I embraced a new path to self-mastery and success. The process was not easy, but it allowed me to break free from the shackles of my past, opening a future filled with possibilities and fulfillment.

Key Insight:

Confronting our coping behaviors and understanding their origins is vital for personal growth. Acknowledging their role but also recognizing when they become hindrances allows us to evolve and embrace a path of self-improvement.

Understanding and Processing Childhood Trauma

Understanding the link between childhood traumas and current behaviors or mindset is crucial. Self-reflection allows us to observe the patterns, beliefs, and behaviors we've adopted and decide which ones we want to keep and which ones we want to eliminate. Fear of spiders can serve as a simple analogy here. As children, our fear might stem from an impactful negative experience, often a physical sensation. As adults, we can view spiders from the perspective of a universal observer and begin to appreciate their existence, thus separating their attributes from our emotional responses.

This same process can be applied to our behaviors or patterns. We need to:

1. Determine the negative pattern we're struggling with.

2.   Affirm the behavior or pattern we'd like to change.

3.   Visualize the moment the behavior or pattern first
     originated, then lovingly assure our younger selves
     that we don't need to continue the pattern.

Childhood is a time when we are largely dependent on others for our physical and mental safety. When our environment fails to provide us this safety, our brains develop coping mechanisms to survive the inflicted pain. However, as adults, we can learn to accept the imperfections of people and our world and use them to strengthen ourselves. Moving past old patterns and freeing ourselves from limiting beliefs and behaviors requires strength, discipline, and tenacity.

Exercises for addressing childhood traumas

Note on Self-Love and Understanding:

 These exercises can bring up painful memories and emotions. It's essential to approach them with the utmost love, understanding, and compassion for yourself, as a loving parent would nurture their child. Be gentle, non-judgmental, and forgiving towards yourself. This journey of self-inquiry should be about healing, gaining wisdom, and embracing the power within you.

Step 1: Identify and Visualize Change

Reflect on any negative pattern you're struggling with in your life right now and write it down. Then, visualize and describe the behavior you'd like to adopt instead, imagining your life free of this harmful pattern.

Step 2: Trace the Origin

Think back to your childhood experiences and identify any events that may have led to this pattern, writing them down to fully acknowledge their impact.

Step 3: Embrace Your Past Self

Close your eyes and visualize yourself going back to the moment where this behavior or pattern first originated. Picture holding your childhood self by the hand or placing an arm around their shoulder. With love and protection, tell them: "My dear [your name], thank you. We survived this. But we don't need this pattern or behavior anymore. We're an adult now, and we can be the person we've always wanted to be."

These exercises guide you on a transformative journey, encouraging you to recognize and release the negative patterns from your past while embracing the future you desire.

Transforming Darkness into Light:

We all go through trauma in life. If we describe trauma as a source of darkness—something that takes away the light in our soul—then overcoming it means transforming that darkness into light. This newfound light, wisdom, and power enable us to help others and recognize when they are grappling with similar darkness or traumas. By healing ourselves, we become a beacon of hope and understanding for those around us.

Chapter 2

EMOTIONAL NEGLECT - THE SILENT DEMON

Emotional neglect refers to instances when an individual, be they a child or an adult, experiences a sense of insignificance— a feeling that their emotions, opinions, or inputs don't matter. This insidious form of neglect often begins in childhood when the adults in a child's life unwittingly dismiss or downplay their emotional responses, expecting them to behave in the same way an adult would. Such attitudes can lead a child to believe they are not important enough to matter, fostering harmful thoughts and behaviors.

Adults, especially those in positions of influence such as parents, teachers, or leaders, carry the responsibility to validate the feelings and emotions of those they interact with. Yet, too often, they shut down a child's emotional response, not recognizing the difference in cognitive or emotional response levels. When children's feelings and thoughts are acknowledged and respected, they learn the concept of mutual respect and empathy. This sort of emotional intelligence is a skill we emphasize in sales and communication training: when someone is angry or frustrated, we seek first to understand and validate their feelings.

One common sign of emotional neglect is apathy, often expressed through the iconic "I don't care" attitude. This viewpoint reflects a protective mechanism: "If my feelings don't matter to others, why should I care about theirs or the world?" This mindset can extend to all areas of life, coloring the individual's worldview and relationships.

In adulthood, emotional neglect can manifest as ruthless, unempathetic behavior, characterized by disregard for others' feelings or indifference to the consequences of their actions. This lack of empathy often stems from an absence of connection and awareness of others' emotions. You might also notice repeated mistakes, indicating a lack of skills for self-correction and learning from failures—skills often developed in a loving, patient environment.

Identifying and Overcoming Emotional Neglect

To identify emotional neglect in your own life, look for patterns of disregard for others 'feelings. Reflect on instances when others made you feel ignored or insignificant. How did it make you feel? Imagine that you already have every material possession and relationship you desire—how would you treat others in this situation? If you were fulfilled and content, you might find yourself behaving in the following ways:

- **Listening More Attentively:** With a satisfied mind, you would likely be more present in your conversations, showing genuine interest in what others have to say.
- **Being More Generous:** Having everything you need, you might be more willing to share your resources, time, and energy to help others in their times of need.
- **Expressing More Compassion:** Feeling content could lead to greater empathy towards others, understanding their feelings, and expressing compassion.
- **Encouraging Others:** You may find joy in lifting others up, offering encouragement, and celebrating their successes.
- **Creating Deeper Connections:** With a contented heart, you might work on building meaningful relationships, focusing on the quality of connections rather than superficial interactions.

Writing down this envisioned behavior and regularly affirming it can be a powerful exercise in transformation. Visualize, affirm, and manifest the person you aspire to be. By recognizing how emotional fulfillment could change your behavior toward others, you can begin to incorporate these positive changes into your life now, regardless of your current circumstances.

Case Study: Emotional Neglect - The Silent Demon

The Experience: Growing up, I faced numerous instances of emotional neglect. Whether it was a parent or teacher abruptly ending a conversation with a dismissive "because I said so" or a sibling or friend choosing their interests over mine, these types of experiences were frequent and painful.

The Impact and Resulting Behavior: These dismissive actions left lasting impressions, instilling a feeling of insignificance and mistrust in relationships. It led to a struggle with self-worth and difficulties in connecting with others, fearing that my emotions would again be disregarded.

Overcoming the Challenge: With time, introspection, and the guidance of supportive mentors, I began to understand that the neglect I experienced was not a reflection of my worth but rather the shortcomings of those around me. I learned to value my emotions and trust myself, recognizing that I deserved respect and consideration.

Transforming Pain into Strength: Through self-compassion and by surrounding myself with empathetic people, I learned to express my emotions freely and advocate for myself. I transformed the pain of neglect into the strength of self-awareness and empathy, empowering me to connect deeply with others and live a more fulfilled life.

Key Insight: Emotional neglect can leave profound scars, but it is possible to heal and grow stronger. By recognizing our worth and nurturing our emotional well-being, we can overcome the silence of neglect and build meaningful, respectful relationships.

Exercises for overcoming emotional neglect

1. Transform Past Experiences:

- View past instances of emotional neglect as catalysts rather than barriers. See them through the lens of love rather than anger. Thanks to the past experience you are able to grow.
- Embrace the lessons learned from these experiences, using them as fuel for personal growth.
- Realize that each experience of emotional neglect or other forms of pain send you to a crossroad where you must choose your response. You will respond based on how well you understand the situation, you empathize with all the individuals involved and how strong your self-control is. These can be trained by simply being present and aware of your feelings and desires at that point. Train to pause yourself and be aware.

2. Visualize Your Ideal Self:

- Imagine the person you aspire to be, considering how you would act if you already had everything you desired.
- Write down the traits and behaviors that define this envisioned version of yourself.
- Affirm this vision daily, using positive statements and visualizations.

3. Prepare for Future Growth:

- Recognize that your past doesn't have to define your future.
- Commit to learning, growing, and triumphing over past experiences.

In the chapters ahead, we'll delve further into strategies to overcome the impacts of emotional neglect, guiding you towards personal growth and fulfillment. Stay with me on this journey as we work together to turn your past experiences into catalysts for positive change.

Chapter 3

PHYSICAL PAIN - THE VISIBLE ENEMY

Physical pain serves as a direct and tangible manifestation of suffering. It can be experienced through an incident like stubbing your toe on a table corner or being attacked by a person or some other creature. These individual painful experiences can, however, lead us to form generalizations about certain objects, living things, or people, categorizing them as visible enemies and triggering our brains to use its power in an incorrect way.

In many instances, the remnants of this physical pain continue to manifest themselves through these generalizations. By continuing to harbor anger towards the source of physical pain, not seeking to understand its nature or motivation, we extend the physical pain into emotional pain. It becomes an arduous enemy that drains our energy reserves, diminishing our ability to think analytically, show kindness, and maintain patience, all of which are also energy-consuming activities in the long run.

As an example, consider the simple act of stubbing your toe against a table. The pain is intense and immediate, often eliciting a reactive emotional response. However, once the pain subsides, it's unnecessary and detrimental to hold on to the anger and resentment towards the table. This kind of continuous emotional pain does nothing but drain us further. Now imagine if that table were a person.

The lasting impact of unaddressed physical pain can create a cycle of negativity that only serves to hinder our growth and well-being. Dealing with physical pain provides a unique opportunity for growth and resilience. It is an inherent part of your life journey, offering you the chance to learn, adapt, and become stronger. Consider activities such as going to the gym or learning a new skill. Initially, it might be a source of stress and physical discomfort, but the consistent effort and enduring the initial pain eventually leads to visible results and progress towards your long-term goals.

Case Study: Turning Pain into Power

The Theme and Personal Experience:

Growing up, I often found myself being bullied by someone older and stronger. This consistent pattern of physical abuse served as a painful and tangible manifestation of suffering in my life.

The Behavior It Led To:

The fear and physical pain from the bullying led me to avoid confrontation altogether. It made me feel weak and vulnerable, creating a mindset where I believed I was incapable of standing up for myself.

The Transformation:

One day, I decided to face the fear and pain head-on. I had enough of being bullied, and the desire to overcome the pain grew stronger than the fear of it. I confronted the bully, endured his punches without a flinch, and eventually pushed him back.

Turning Into Strength:

This experience was more than just standing up to a bully; it was about using physical pain as a catalyst to become mentally stronger. I transformed the painful experience into a lesson of resilience and courage. I learned that facing pain, understanding its nature, and overcoming it can lead to immense personal growth.

Key Insights:

The transformation from a victim of physical pain to a victor over it illustrates the power of mindset and determination. By confronting the source of pain and transforming it into strength, we can break free from what once held us captive and move forward to a life of empowerment and confidence.

Exercises for managing physical pain

Step 1: Cultivate Acceptance

Start by acknowledging the presence of physical pain without judgment. Accept the pain as a sensation rather than an enemy, deepening your connection with your body.

Step 2: Direct Attention to the Source

Direct your mind towards the source of the pain, distinguishing between the natural physical reactions and any emotional or judgmental responses you may have. Notice the difference and observe how you feel about the pain.

Step 3: Identify and Analyze Reactions

Through introspective exercises, identify the sources of your reactions to pain. Ask yourself whether these reactions are serving you or if you need to retrain your responses to pain. Write down your insights and decide on ways to modify your perceptions if necessary.

Step 4: Transform Pain into a Teacher

Reflect on how pain can be transformed from an enemy into a teacher. Understand its origins, its influence on your perceptions, and the surprising ways it can make you stronger. See pain as an opportunity for growth and learning.

Note on Perspective:

Enduring physical pain isn't about inviting needless suffering into our lives. It's about comprehending its origins, its influence on our thoughts and emotions, and using it as a tool for personal growth and resilience.

Further Exploration:

Consider exploring literature on pain management and the psychology of pain perception to enhance your understanding of these concepts. This additional reading can provide valuable insights and techniques for dealing with physical pain in your daily life.

By working through these exercises, you're not only learning to manage physical pain but also embracing it as a part of your journey toward self-mastery and empowerment.

Chapter 4

FROM DECEIT TO DETERMINATION

Overcoming betrayal and lies

Deceit, as we understand it in this context, is not just about lies or dishonesty. It's about the crushing disappointment and feelings of betrayal when someone we relied on for our happiness or well-being fails us or acts contrary to our expectations. Such reliance on others can often lead to disappointment, particularly when expectations are not met. This can occur at any stage of life, but it is especially impactful when we are young. Childhood experiences such as a friend not choosing you for their team as promised, a sibling repeatedly breaking a promise or neglecting you, or someone unexpectedly hurting you physically or emotionally, can have long-lasting effects.

Such experiences can lead to intense feelings of sadness, anger, and disappointment, and even result in trust issues. In an attempt to shield ourselves from further pain, we may become overly independent and self-reliant, always expecting disappointment as a way to protect our emotional well-being. This can also affect our ability to be vulnerable in relationships, as we may fear opening ourselves up to potential hurt.

However, there is a path from this deceit to determination. While the energy derived from the feeling of betrayal is powerful, it's crucial to channel it positively, towards self-improvement and growth. This shift in mindset can transform the pain of deceit into the power of determination.

As we journey through life, our goal should be to source happiness from within ourselves, rather than relying on others. By striving to only rely on what we can control, which is ourselves, we build a more resilient and self-sufficient sense of joy that's less prone to being shaken by external circumstances. This self-reliance enables us to better manage disappointment and helps in our transformation from deceit to determination.

Case Study: Turning Betrayal into Wisdom

Example of Personal Experience: A few years ago, I was betrayed by a close friend and mentor during a business negotiation, leading to a draining lawsuit. This occurred during one of the most challenging times of my life, amid the COVID pandemic and my wife's pregnancy.

Dealing with Deceit: The pain of deceit was intensified by the overall stress of the situation, but I was determined to fight for my rights and clear my name. I recognized that relying on others for success or happiness could lead to disappointment, and I chose to rely on myself instead.

Behavior It Led To: The betrayal ignited a determination within me, pushing me to take control of the situation. Rather than seeing it as a setback, I viewed it as a learning opportunity, focusing on what I could control – myself.

Key Insight - Deceit to Determination: Despite the hardship, I used this experience as a source of strength and wisdom, learning more than I had in the previous five years as a business owner. I discovered the importance of sourcing happiness and 'my next move' from within, not relying on others, thus avoiding unmet expectations, disappointments and following paths which are not mine. The experience not only strengthened me as a person but also made me a wiser businessman and friend.

Through this journey, I transformed a moment of deceit into a determination that fueled my growth, showing that even in betrayal, valuable lessons can be learned, and strength can be found.

Exercises for overcoming the pain of deceit

Step 1: Acknowledge Your Feelings

Begin by acknowledging the moments when you felt neglected, overlooked, or betrayed. Write them down to gain clarity on your emotions.

Step 2: Choose Trusted Loved Ones for Open Communication

Identify the closest and most trusted friends or family members with whom you'd like to discuss your feelings. Be selective, choosing those who can offer support and understanding. Perhaps you don't have any such person in your family or group of friends. In that case, talk to a professional. It's essential to trust your instincts to determine whether the professional you're going to see is a right fit. When sharing personal stories, whether with friends, family, or even a professional, always follow your instincts until you find someone who feels right for you. A professional should maintain confidentiality, referring you to other healthcare professionals only when necessary for your safety.

Step 3: Schedule a Time to Talk or Seek Self-Understanding

If the person who has deceived or betrayed you is open to conversation, set up a time to talk, expressing your feelings without using harsh words that may strain the relationship. If they are not open to communication or you feel that talking to them would not be beneficial, focus instead on self-reflection and understanding. Explore your feelings, emotions, and reactions related to the betrayal. Engage in activities that promote healing, such as journaling, meditation, or seeking professional guidance if needed. The goal is to understand and come to terms with the betrayal, whether through direct communication or personal growth, always emphasizing self-care and emotional well-being.

Step 3-1: Express Your Feelings with Care

If your conversation takes place, articulate your feelings calmly and with empathy. Focus on being honest without straining the relationship. Your goal is to ensure your feelings are acknowledged, not necessarily to gain acceptance.

Step 4: Reflect on Your Chosen 'Family'

Reflect on the relationships that matter most to you, recognizing that while you can't choose your blood relatives, you have the power to choose your friends and form your own supportive 'family'.

Note on Perspective:

Remember Friedrich Nietzsche's words: "What does not kill me, makes me stronger." Use this as a mantra to remind yourself that the strength to overcome deceit and foster determination lies within you.

These exercises are designed to guide you through a challenging but essential process of healing and empowerment. By embracing open communication and self-reflection, you can transform the pain of deceit into a steppingstone toward a more resilient and fulfilled life.

Chapter 5

THE BONDS OF MANIPULATION

Manipulation is not merely a tactic of control but a suffocating bond that entraps individuals, exploiting their innate desire to help others. Other examples of manipulation include leveraging someone's guilt or insecurities, playing on their fears, utilizing deceptive charm or flattery, creating a false sense of urgency or scarcity, or even feigning helplessness or playing the victim to achieve a hidden agenda. These methods can be used to manipulate others in various relationships and contexts, from personal friendships and romantic relationships to professional interactions and societal dynamics.

This manipulative entrapment often stems from childhood experiences where one may have been a caretaker for parents or siblings, fostering a sense of duty that can be twisted and leveraged against them. Manipulators identify these vulnerabilities and use feelings of guilt, anger, or fear to coerce actions that might be harmful physically, mentally, or spiritually. Such manipulation stunts growth and hinders the realization of one's true, powerful, and free-minded self.

In the context of this book, "Defeat Your Demons," these manipulative tactics can lead to parasitic relationships, positioning manipulation as one of the sinister demons that must be confronted and overcome.

Breaking Free from Manipulative Relationships

1. **Intuitive Understanding**: Cultivate an intuitive connection with your mind to discern what feels "right." Listen to your gut feeling and question the intention behind information.

2. **Independence**: Strive for a self-sufficient environment, especially financially. If immediate freedom isn't possible, begin privately putting things in place to break free. Get out and go somewhere safe as fast as possible. Be sure able people you can trust know what you're doing and why. It helps to have support.

3. **Survival Mindset**: Identify your essential needs and cut out unnecessary elements, including harmful relationships.

Research and learn from others' experiences, acquiring wisdom to discern false intent.

4. **Say "No"**: Learn to assertively say "no." *Saying no to others is saying yes to yourself.* Put yourself first and recognize that true love doesn't involve manipulation.

Case Study: Escaping the Snare of Manipulation

Background:

A compassionate and hard-working student of mine, who we'll call 'Jane' to protect her identity, always put others first. As a child, she played the caretaker role in her family, looking after her younger siblings. This sense of duty had been deeply ingrained in her from an early age.

Challenge:

In her late 20s, Jane entered a romantic relationship with Tom, who initially appeared charming and caring. Over time, Tom began to manipulate Jane, leveraging her guilt and insecurities, creating a false sense of urgency around his needs, and playing on her fears.

Tom's manipulative behavior started subtly, often disguised as affection or concern. But as the relationship progressed, his demands became more controlling. He exploited Jane's desire to help others, manipulating her financially and emotionally.

Approach:

Jane began to feel trapped, recognizing that the relationship was becoming toxic. Inspired by the principles outlined in "Defeat Your Demons," she decided to take the following steps:

1. **Intuitive Understanding:** Jane started listening to her gut feelings, questioning Tom's intentions, and realizing that his actions didn't align with genuine love.

2. **Independence:** She began working towards financial independence, setting aside funds privately to secure her future. She confided in trusted friends, explaining her situation and gaining their support.

3. **Survival Mindset:** Jane researched manipulation and learned from others' experiences, understanding the patterns and tactics Tom was using against her.

4. **Say "No":** Jane started to assert herself, firmly saying "no" to Tom's unreasonable demands. This was a significant step in reclaiming her power and control over her life.

Outcome:

With determination and the support of friends, Jane managed to break free from the manipulative relationship. It was a painful journey, but she emerged stronger, more self-aware, and more empowered. Jane's experience serves as a testament to the fact that one can transform pain from an enemy into a teacher.

Key Insights:

Jane's story is a powerful example of how manipulative bonds can entrap even the most caring and selfless individuals. By following the principles of intuitive understanding, independence, survival mindset, and assertiveness, one can break free from these suffocating bonds and foster personal growth and fulfillment. Her journey illustrates the need to recognize and confront the demons of manipulation, transcending them to achieve true self-mastery.

Exercises to break free from manipulative bonds

1. **Practice Saying "No"**: Create scenarios where you might typically feel pressured or manipulated. Practice saying "no" and affirm your right to prioritize yourself.

2. **Intuitive Journaling**: Keep a daily journal noting when something doesn't feel right. Reflect on these situations and try to identify patterns or underlying intentions.

3. **Financial Independence Plan:** If financial manipulation is a concern, outline a step-by-step plan to achieve financial independence. Seek professional advice if needed.

4. **Self-love and Care Routine**: Develop a routine that prioritizes your well-being. Embrace self-love, recognizing that those who truly care for you will not seek to manipulate you.

5. **Empower Yourself Physically:** Choose to engage in physical activities like going to the gym, dance classes, or practicing a martial art. Doing these or similar bodily activities independently from any relationship promotes self-awareness of your body and mind. By empowering yourself through the discipline of practicing bodily exercise, you start realizing inner strength, self-worth, and gain valuable friendships, breaking free from unhealthy relationships and habits.

Manipulation is a complex and painful experience, but the strength to overcome it is within your reach. Remember that wisdom is gained through both painful and joyous experiences. Embrace the lessons and allow them to guide you to a healthier, freer life.

Chapter 6

CORPORATE GIANTS - THE GOLIATHS OF OUR TIME

Recognizing and Standing Up to Powerful Entities

Corporate giants are master manipulators, exploiting human psychology to create a connection between their products and our desires and behaviors. Through advertising and clever marketing, they can create a perceived need for products that might not be essential, associating them with status, happiness, or success.

They exploit our vulnerabilities by using targeted advertising and leveraging data analytics, showing us personalized content that resonates with our preferences and weaknesses. Celebrities and influencers are roped in to endorse products, creating a sense of aspiration and social validation. Many products are intentionally designed to be addictive, keeping users engaged for hours or encouraging unhealthy cravings.

Misleading information and pseudoscience are often employed to create a false perception of their products, with terms like "natural" or "healthy" masking the reality. Fear and scarcity are leveraged to instill urgency and drive impulsive buying, while sales strategies encourage overconsumption of potentially unhealthy products.

Children are not spared, with corporations targeting them through colorful and attractive advertising to shape their preferences early on. Some entities even undermine regulations that would protect consumer interests, lobbying against ethical considerations.

Notably, this manipulative entrapment goes further, distancing people from their natural selves and the natural world. The influence of these corporate giants can lead to a dependency on chemicals, products, or foods that are harmful rather than healthy, natural, or beneficial. This overreliance on artificial substances and processed goods can thin our connection to our innate nature and the natural environment that we are born to live in.

Some of these goliaths also manipulate their image regarding environmental and societal impact, portraying themselves as responsible through greenwashing and CSR activities, diverting attention from potentially harmful practices.

In essence, the tactics employed by these corporate Goliaths not only shape our desires and behaviors but can also estrange us from our natural selves. Understanding and resisting their influence is vital for maintaining a connection to what's genuinely beneficial for us, allowing for conscious and responsible consumer choices.

Impact on Individuals and Society

Corporate giants contribute to a range of consequences that reverberate through both individual lives and the fabric of society. Their peddling of processed and low-quality products is more than a mere business strategy; it's a health crisis, leading to obesity, chronic diseases, and a growing disconnect from our natural selves.

These behemoths do not only damage physical well-being but also fuel economic inequalities. By offering cheap, addictive products, they strategically target lower-income households, exacerbating economic disparities and trapping vulnerable communities in cycles of dependency on artificial substances and processed goods.

Furthermore, their influence extends into the cultural sphere, where they promote materialism, consumerism, and short-term pleasure-seeking. Such values erode deeper connections to oneself and others, thinning the ties to our innate nature and the natural environment. Through manipulative marketing strategies and insidious psychological tactics, they are not only reshaping individual desires but also transforming the collective consciousness, leading us away from health, equality, and authentic human connection.

Case Study: Jeffrey, the Inspiring Entrepreneur

Background:

Jeffrey, a self-made millionaire and successful entrepreneur, once found himself deeply entrenched in the web of corporate influence. Like many, he was unknowingly manipulated by the deceptive practices of large companies that prioritize profit over well-being.

Challenge:

Upon achieving business success, Jeffrey began to understand how these corporate giants were manipulating his desires and encouraging a dependence on artificial and harmful products. He recognized that his connection to his natural self and the environment had been weakened, and he was determined to change.

Action:

Jeffrey took conscious control of his choices, seeking out products and practices that were in alignment with his values and well-being. He actively avoided the seductive allure of materialism promoted by these companies, instead opting for healthy, natural, and genuinely beneficial alternatives.

Outcome:

Jeffrey's deliberate choices led him to a life where he was no longer controlled by corporate influence. He reconnected with his natural self and found true satisfaction in his decisions. His family followed his lead, and together they embraced a lifestyle that prioritized health, nature, and genuine fulfillment.

Reflection:

Jeffrey's story is a testament to the power of awareness and the ability to break free from the influence of corporate giants. It serves as an inspiring example for others, showing that success and fulfillment lie in authenticity and alignment with one's true self, rather than in the hollow promises of manipulative corporations. His journey emphasizes the importance of critical thinking and personal empowerment in overcoming the seemingly insurmountable Goliaths of our time.

Exercises - standing up to corporate giants

1. Reconnect with Nature: Embrace a more natural lifestyle by focusing on whole, organic foods, and engaging all your senses. Spend a week connecting with nature through activities like tasting natural foods, listening to the sounds of the earth, feeling different textures, and walking in natural environments such as forests, beaches, and grasslands. Journal your experiences to reflect on how they make you feel.

2. Educate Yourself and Cultivate Awareness: Investigate the techniques used in advertising and corporate manipulations. Analyze your consumption patterns and identify products that you may be addicted to. Research and find healthier alternatives or discover the strength within to stop or moderate your use.

3. Pursue Financial Independence: Control over your finances can break the grip of corporate influence. Develop a plan to manage your money and align your investments with your values. Consider that financial stability can enable you to afford healthy foods, pursue beneficial habits, and live in an environment more in tune with nature.

4. Assess and Adjust Consumption Habits: Reflect on your daily consumption habits. Are there areas where corporate influence is guiding your choices? Work on replacing those products with healthier alternatives that align with your values and support your well-being.

These strategies are designed to empower you to recognize and resist the manipulations of corporate giants. Through understanding their tactics, reconnecting with your natural self, and making conscious, informed choices, you can forge a path to a healthier, more balanced life. Embrace these practices as a guide to standing up to the Goliaths of our time and reclaiming control over your life.

5. Analyze Attention Grabbers: Be mindful of how your attention is seized or maintained by external elements, particularly electronic devices, advertisements, or corporate tools. Pay close attention to what lures you in when you are tired or emotionally charged. Recognize that many products and services, including applications like social media, TV programs, and games, are crafted to exploit the distress you may be feeling, providing a temporary relief from stress or fatigue. Investigate how these mediums are constructed and what makes them appealing. Research their underlying structures to understand how they operate. By discerning their mechanisms, you can either position yourself as a co-creator of content or learn to ignore them altogether, liberating yourself from their hold.

By integrating this practice into your daily routine, you can heighten your awareness of the subtle ways in which corporate influences permeate your life. This newfound understanding empowers you to make conscious choices, giving you the agency to break free from manipulative tactics and align more closely with your values and authentic self.

Chapter 7

THE COMFORT TRAP - THE LURE OF INSTANT GRATIFICATION

The comfort trap is a pervasive challenge in modern life, symbolizing the battle between short-term gratification desires and long-term goals. We live in an age where immediate pleasure is not only accessible but encouraged, from fast food to binge-watching television series. These temptations are alluring because they offer a quick reward, a fleeting sense of satisfaction that requires little to no effort.

Achieving long-term goals, on the other hand, often requires enduring discomfort, discipline, and delayed gratification. Whether it's pursuing a fitness regimen, building a career, or nurturing meaningful relationships, the path to genuine fulfillment is rarely easy or immediate. It demands persistence, patience, and a willingness to face challenges and setbacks.

Yet, the pull towards immediate pleasure is strong and often masquerades as comfort. The allure of the comfort trap lies in its deceptive simplicity; it seems easier to choose what's readily available and pleasurable now over what may seem abstract and distant in the future.

Resisting these temptations and navigating past the comfort trap leads to long-lasting happiness and a sense of accomplishment. It fosters personal growth, integrity, and a deeper connection to one's true aspirations. The mastery of self-control in the face of immediate pleasures helps in aligning actions with values and in building a life that resonates with purpose and meaning.

In "The Comfort Trap - The Lure of Instant Gratification," this chapter will explore the various facets of this struggle, offering insights, case studies, and strategies to recognize and overcome the comfort trap, guiding readers towards a life rich with fulfillment, growth, and enduring joy.

Understanding the inner workings of the Comfort Trap

The comfort trap is more than a mere struggle between desires and goals; it's a complex interplay within our minds, rooted in the natural human tendency to seek pleasure and avoid discomfort. This instinctive behavior often conflicts with our ability to think rationally and plan for the future.

This internal struggle manifests in daily decisions and choices, creating a tension between actions that offer immediate pleasure and those that align with our long-term goals and values. Whether it's a subtle force nudging us toward the easier path or a powerful urge demanding immediate satisfaction, the comfort trap is constantly at play.

Understanding this dynamic is key to overcoming the comfort trap. By recognizing the pull between our immediate desires and our rational thinking, we can cultivate the strength to choose actions that support our lasting objectives, even if they feel uncomfortable or challenging initially. By reflecting on our personal experiences, seeking insights from our inner thoughts, and learning from our successes and failures, we can navigate this complex landscape. This self-awareness and mindfulness empowers us to make choices that lead to genuine fulfillment and success, free from the lure of instant gratification.

Recognizing the Trap

The comfort trap is a deceptive snare that can manifest itself in various aspects of our daily lives. It's not just in behaviors like stress-eating, where the pursuit of immediate pleasure leads to later guilt and disrupts our long-term objectives. This trap also ensnares us in other recognizable ways:

- **Procrastination**: Putting off essential tasks for the allure of relaxing or engaging in entertainment can hinder our progress towards significant life goals.
- **Excessive Spending**: The immediate satisfaction of buying something new might feel good momentarily but can lead to financial instability in the long run.
- **Unhealthy Relationships**: Staying in a familiar but toxic relationship might feel comfortable for the moment but can hinder personal growth and emotional well-being.
- **Overindulging in Screen Time**: Spending hours on social media or binge-watching television series might provide instant entertainment but can rob us of time to pursue hobbies, personal development, or meaningful connections with others.

Recognizing these patterns allows us to see beyond the immediate allure of comfort. It challenges us to endure temporary discomfort, resist temptations, and focus on achieving more sustainable, long-term contentment. By understanding the diverse ways the comfort trap can manifest in our lives, we are better equipped to align our actions with our true goals and values, leading to a more fulfilling life.

Case Study: Breaking Free from the Comfort Trap

Introduction :

In a 12-week coaching program, a client sought help to lose weight and build self-confidence but soon discovered the insidious lure of the comfort trap. The struggle against instant gratification became a constant battle, revealing the deeper issues underlying the temptation to succumb to immediate pleasure.

Challenges and Struggles:

The journey was filled with challenges, as the comfort of old habits beckoned. The temptation to indulge in unhealthy snacks, to fall back into the familiar lifestyle they were used to, and to skip training sessions was a constant struggle. The battle was between the person they once were and the person they aspired to become.

Process of Discovery and Growth:

Guided by coaching, the client delved into their psyche to uncover the coping mechanisms that manifested as a craving for ease. They realized that these habits acted as shields against stress and the fear of failure. Overcoming the temptation to fall back into the "comfort zone" demanded tremendous strength, endurance, and discipline.

Turning Points and Achievements:

Though the process was fraught with frustration, doubt, and temptation, the client's commitment to self and vision of the future kept them on track. Slowly, the struggles transformed into lessons, and the client grew stronger and more resilient. They noticed changes not only in their body but also in their mind, feeling empowered and confident like never before.

Beyond Transformation:

By the end of the program, the client had transcended their initial goal, breaking free from the comfort trap and rejecting the influences that sought to keep them confined. The transformation was not just physical but mental and emotional, revealing the unbreakable bond between persistence, introspection, and success. The metamorphosis was complete, and the client emerged with an impenetrable sense of self, ready to embrace long-term gratification.

This case study illuminates the complex nature of the comfort trap and underscores the necessity of recognizing and overcoming its allure. It's a testament to our human capacity to grow, change, and triumph over the deceptively comforting habits that can hinder our true potential.

Exercises - mapping your transformation

- **Long-Term Commitment:** Begin by setting goals that range from 12 weeks to a year. Recognize that habits don't change overnight, especially if you've been practicing them for years. Break down these long-term aspirations into monthly and weekly milestones and create a structured plan to follow.
- **Documenting the Challenges:** Keep a journal of your journey. Note the short-term comforts that tempt you along the way and evaluate their impact on your

progress. Understand why these habits appeal to you and either find substitutes or endure the discomfort until new habits take root. Remember, it's a process like learning to drive a car; it takes practice and repetition.

- **Envisioning Your Success:** Visualize the person you want to be and the joy of achieving your goals. Act as if you're already there and make affirmations a daily practice. This mental rehearsal helps align your subconscious mind with your goals and can empower you to overcome the obstacles you'll face.

Embracing the New You

Breaking free from the comfort trap requires more than just determination; it needs a conscious understanding of how your brain and body learn. Allow yourself the time, consistency, and frequency needed for new behaviors to become second nature. The pursuit of immediate pleasure can be enticing, but focusing on long-term happiness leads to sustainable transformation. Although the journey might feel challenging, the rewards are profound and life changing. By giving yourself the time and the tools to reprogram, you unlock the door to a new, empowered you.

Chapter 8

DISCIPLINE - THE ULTIMATE WEAPON

Discipline: The Ultimate Weapon for Success

Discipline is far more than self-control; it's an art, a skill, and a weapon. As the power to set a goal and relentlessly pursue it, resisting distractions, temptations, or momentary weaknesses, discipline is the ultimate weapon in achieving success. Whether you're striving to overcome harmful habits, aiming to grow stronger physically or mentally, or working towards professional accomplishments, discipline is the key.

Why Discipline is Unmatched

- **Effort and Perseverance:** Building discipline often starts with tasks that require true effort, like adhering to a consistent gym routine. When you push through fatigue, discomfort, or a lack of motivation, you're forging the weapon of discipline.

- **Adherence to a Plan:** Sticking to a program, be it self-created or guided by a trainer, necessitates discipline. It's tempting to stray and fall into the comfort trap, but a disciplined approach ensures you stay the course, making your goals attainable.

- **Creating Routine and Habit:** Commitment to a routine reinforces discipline. By continually choosing your goal over temporary pleasures, you make discipline a natural part of your life.

- **Physical and Mental Empowerment:** Activities like weightlifting or practicing martial arts not only build physical strength but also demonstrate your perseverance. The transformation of your body becomes a tangible representation of the strength of your mind.

Unleashing Discipline in All Aspects of Life

Once you achieve discipline in one area, such as maintaining a regular fitness regimen, this ultimate weapon can be applied to various other goals. The discipline forged in the gym becomes a metaphor for life, empowering you to take control, set firm boundaries, and follow through with every intention.

The true beauty of discipline lies in its adaptability. You can wield it in your career, relationships, personal development, or any area that requires steadfast determination and focus. It's not about mere control but about mastery, understanding, and empowerment.

Later, in the section of exercises, we will explore practical ways to cultivate discipline and utilize it as your ultimate weapon in all aspects of life. This journey is about transforming not only your actions but your mindset, equipping you with the tools to conquer challenges and create a life of fulfillment and success.

Case Study: The Power of Discipline

James's Struggle and Decision to Change

James, a young professional, found himself stuck in a rut. Struggling with weight management and haunted by constant procrastination at work, he realized that he needed to make a change. His desire for success both physically and professionally led him to the ultimate weapon: discipline.

Phase One - Forging the Weapon: Building Discipline in the Gym

James committed to a consistent gym routine, hitting the weights 3-4 times a week, regardless of temptations and fatigue. Every push, pull, and lift was not just a physical challenge but a mental one, sculpting his discipline.

Phase Two - Wielding the Weapon: Applying Discipline to His Career

The discipline James nurtured in the gym became a tool he could wield in other aspects of his life. He applied the same dedication and perseverance to his work, setting clear goals, following through, and transforming his once stagnant career.

Phase Three - Mastery and Maintenance: Sustaining Discipline in Life

But James's story didn't end there. He continued his disciplined approach, maintaining his gym routine, and persistently excelling in his career. The discipline had become more than a skill; it was now a part of his very being.

The Transformation: From Struggle to Success

James's journey demonstrates the incredible potential of discipline. Once cultivated and mastered, it served as a powerful weapon in various areas of his life. His transformation was not just physical or professional but a complete metamorphosis that revealed the empowering force of discipline. James broke free from his struggles, and with his newly forged weapon, he unlocked a life of success, fulfillment, and control. His story is a testament to the adaptability, strength, and ultimate power of discipline, inspiring us all to take the reins and shape our own destiny.

Exercises: Sculpting Your Ultimate Weapon - Discipline

1. **Forge Your Path: Define Clear, Tangible Goals**

   ➢ **What's Your Destination?** Pinpoint what you want to achieve in different areas of your life.

   ➢ **The Roadmap:** Create a step-by-step plan, breaking down the journey into manageable pieces. If you're unsure, don't hesitate to seek professional guidance.

2. **Building Discipline: Commit to a Routine**

   ➢ **Choose Your Arena:** Select an activity that demands discipline, such as regular gym visits or a martial art.

   ➢ **Stay Consistent:** Make a schedule and stick to it, turning practice into a habitual part of your life.

3. **Wield Your Weapon: Apply Discipline in Various Areas**

   ➢ **Spread Your Wings:** Use the discipline gained in one area to tackle other aspects of life.

   ➢ **Learn from the Struggle:** Recognize that each challenge faced and overcome sharpens your skill.

4. **Track, Reflect, and Grow: Assessing Progress**

   ➢ **Measure Your Steps:** Regularly track your progress, noting successes and areas for improvement.

   ➢ **Reflect on the Journey:** Journal or discuss your experiences to understand how you're growing.

5. Accountability and Support: Find a Discipline Partner

> **Share the Path:** Engage with friends or trainers who can keep you accountable and motivated.

6. The Joy of Mastery: Celebrate Achievements, Big and Small

> **Recognize Efforts:** Honor every step forward, big or small.
> **Fuel the Fire:** Use your successes as momentum to keep moving forward, maintaining, and expanding your discipline.

The Power of Discipline: A Lifelong Journey

Discipline is more than a tool; it's a skill, a mindset, an ultimate weapon that can transform every aspect of life. Whether you're overcoming obstacles, striving for personal growth, or building a foundation for success, the path of discipline is not just a journey but a lifelong commitment. It may be challenging, but the rewards are immense, fulfilling, and empowering. By understanding its power, committing to practice, and applying this ultimate weapon, you unlock a life of limitless potential. The choice, the power, and the weapon are in your hands.

Chapter 9

EMOTIONAL RESILIENCE - THE INDOMITABLE SPIRIT

The Power of Emotions

We are all born with emotions and emotional responses, profound tools that can serve as sources of strength or become overwhelming forces. Emotions are neither inherently good nor bad, but rather complex mechanisms that connect us to our human experience.

Anger: Often viewed negatively, anger possesses immense strength. It can neutralize fear, prompt action, and fuel determination when appropriately harnessed. Misdirected, it can lead to destruction and regret, but when controlled, it can be a catalyst for positive change.

Sadness: Far from a sign of weakness, sadness fosters empathy, compassion, and reflection. It allows us to connect with others' pain and can lead to deeper understanding and healing. While excessive sadness may lead to depression, embracing sadness at appropriate times can enrich our emotional depth.

Happiness: This emotion empowers, energizes, and uplifts us. Happiness enhances creativity, strengthens relationships, and promotes well-being. Rather than a fleeting pleasure, true happiness derives from a sense of purpose, fulfillment, and connection with others.

Fear: Fear serves as a natural warning system, guiding us away from potential harm. While paralyzing when disproportionate, a healthy sense of fear promotes caution and helps us make informed decisions. Understanding and controlling fear can turn it into a guide rather than an obstacle.

Love: More than just a romantic feeling, love embodies connection, care, and acceptance. It bonds families, friendships, and communities, promoting cooperation and understanding. Love enriches our lives, providing a sense of belonging and security.

Disgust: Often overlooked, disgust serves as a protective mechanism, guiding us away from things that could be harmful or toxic. It influences our choices in food, relationships, and environments, helping us maintain our well-being.

Emotions are like fire; they can cook our food or set the entire forest ablaze. Learning to recognize, understand, and control our emotions is vital in harnessing their power. In many cultures and societal structures, we might be incorrectly encouraged to suppress emotions or see them as weakness. However, it's by controlling them and using them at appropriate times and in proportionate levels that we can access the strength they grant. Emotions are central to being human, and when embraced and guided, they become powerful allies on our journey through life.

Cultivating Emotional Strength and Flexibility

The Path to the Indomitable Spirit

Emotional strength and flexibility aren't just about reacting to feelings in the moment; they're about understanding the underlying complexities and learning to navigate them effectively. This awareness enables us to grow and adapt, responding to life's challenges with grace and wisdom.

Understanding emotional reactions means *recognizing triggers*, often linked to unresolved or unaccepted situations from our past, leading to inappropriate or exaggerated responses in adulthood. Acknowledging these underlying causes is the first step towards emotional mastery.

Training emotional awareness involves techniques such as meditation, mindfulness, and visualization. These practices help us connect deeply with our emotions, allowing us to control reactions rather than be controlled by them.

Emotions like anger, fear, or anxiety can be managed through focused exercises, leading to better emotional regulation. Specific practices can help us gain control over these feelings, enabling appropriate and positive responses. You will find such exercises later in this chapter.

Emotional flexibility is about adaptability and resilience. It means learning to respond to situations with values and context in mind, rather than reacting out of habit or impulse. This approach fosters an adaptable and balanced response to various emotional challenges.

Compassion and empathy play a vital role in emotional strength, softening our responses and deepening connections with others. They teach us to respond with kindness and understanding, even when faced with challenging emotions.

Creating a supportive environment with friends, family, or professionals can foster emotional growth. Sharing the emotional journey with others can provide insights and encouragement, enhancing emotional strength and flexibility.

Emotional resilience is not a rigid state but a dynamic and evolving quality, reflecting continuous growth and learning. Cultivating these traits unlocks inner potential, leading to a more empowered and authentic self. Far from a sign of weakness, emotional strength and flexibility are the cornerstones of an indomitable spirit, equipping us to face life's trials with courage and determination.

Case Study: Sylvia's Transformation – Embracing Emotional Strength and Flexibility

Meet Sylvia, a dedicated professional who had long struggled with uncontrolled anger and emotional rigidity. Her emotional responses were akin to a wildfire – unpredictable and destructive. These challenges not only affected her relationships but also hindered her professional growth.

Phase One - Understanding Emotional Triggers: Sylvia's journey began with acknowledging her underlying emotional triggers. These were often linked to unresolved issues from her past, leading to inappropriate reactions in her adult life. Recognizing these triggers was her first step towards transformation.

Phase Two - Training Emotional Awareness: Determined to change, Sylvia embarked on a path of self-discovery and empowerment. She started practicing emotional visualization exercises, as we will explore later in this chapter, meditating daily, and attending training courses and seminars focused on emotional regulation and empowerment. These practices, akin to the exercises and teachings in this book, helped Sylvia connect deeply with her emotions. She learned to control her reactions rather than being controlled by them, transforming her life through the mastery of emotional awareness.

Phase Three - Cultivating Emotional Flexibility: Sylvia's focused exercises led to better emotional regulation. She learned to respond to situations with adaptability and resilience. Her responses became more balanced, reflecting her values and context rather than reacting out of habit or impulse.

Phase Four - Building Compassion and Empathy: Along her journey, Sylvia fostered compassion and empathy, softening her responses, and deepening her connections with herself and others. She began to respond with kindness and understanding, even when faced with challenging emotions.

Phase Five - Creating a Supportive Environment: Sylvia also worked on creating a supportive environment with friends, family, and professionals. Sharing her emotional journey with others provided insights and encouragement, further enhancing her emotional strength and flexibility.

Sylvia's Transformation: Sylvia's dedication to understanding and controlling her emotions transformed her life. She could handle criticism without anger, connect with people through empathy, and foster joy in her life. Her newfound emotional strength and flexibility not only turned her personal and professional life around but made her a symbol of the power of emotional resilience in the modern world. Her journey illustrates that emotional resilience is a dynamic quality, reflecting continuous growth and learning. Sylvia's story is a testament to the indomitable spirit within us all, ready to be unleashed through understanding, practice, and perseverance.

Exercises:

1. **Anger Control Exercise**: This exercise helps you gain control over anger, one of the most potentially destructive emotions.

   ➢ To begin, affirm that you are in full control as the owner of your mind and emotions.

   ➢ Visualize your anger levels on a scale from 1 to 10. Start by counting out loud for yourself from 1 to 10. With each number, feel the anger increasing slightly. Pay attention to the physical changes that occur with each number, such as furrowing your eyebrows, clenching your hands, tightening your jaw, or a lowering of your voice tone. However, try not to remain at one level for more than 10 seconds, especially when starting with this exercise. Afterwards, practice counting back down to 0 to calm yourself down.

   An interesting point to note is that feelings of fear often decrease as you become angrier. At the same time, the urge to take action increases the angrier you become. This is valuable information about yourself. It confirms that anger can empower you to act without being paralyzed by the fear of failure.

   This illustrates the importance of managing your anger and using it as a source of energy for positive actions. Just as fire can both destroy a forest and warm a living room, anger can be destructive if not controlled. However, when used in a focused and responsible manner, it can be a powerful catalyst for positive change and action. It's up to you to decide how to channel this potent emotion: as a destructive flame or as a hum of warmth and light.

➤ Repeat this exercise several times a week by yourself or with a trusted partner if possible.

➤ If you doubt your ability to complete this exercise, seek help from a highly skilled martial arts instructor who specializes in emotional control or explore my personal training programs.

2. **Daily Emotional Reflection**: Create a journal dedicated to documenting and reflecting on your daily emotional experiences. Understand what triggers certain feelings, how you act upon them, and how you might channel them in more constructive ways. Affirm any negative habit you want to transform into a positive one by writing it down or saying it aloud as many times as you feel necessary for a couple of minutes.

3. **Mindful Awareness Meditation**: Dedicate time each day to mindfulness meditation, focusing on sensations and breathing. This practice sharpens your awareness of emerging emotions, allowing for more conscious and controlled responses. Choose the right environment for this exercise. It should be done in an environment that stimulates 'peace of mind,' such as natural outdoor environments like forests, valleys, or the beach, or you can do this indoors with soft accompanying music that contains no words.

4. **Compassion and Empathy Engagement:** Engage with people around you, aiming to understand their feelings and viewpoints without judgment. Through active listening and empathy, you can cultivate emotional flexibility and deeper connections with others. Try making it a daily practice to consciously empathize with friends, family, or even strangers during a conversation. Be aware of any inclination to want to respond emotionally and control any impulse to give your conversational partner the space for their feelings to be heard without your emotional reaction to it. This practice will lead to better control of emotional responses and the ability to apply them during moments when you deem them necessary and appropriate.

Emotional resilience is a dynamic and ongoing process. The power to navigate life's complexities with grace and confidence lies in the continuous practice of understanding, controlling, and employing our emotions. By embracing these exercises, you can cultivate the strength and flexibility needed to face challenges with an indomitable spirit.

Personalized Emotional Empowerment Training: If you seek to deepen your mastery over emotional resilience, consider exploring specialized training programs or courses on emotional regulation and empowerment. As a professional in this area, I understand how this personalized guidance can be tailored to your unique needs and challenges. Such one-on-one coaching may add further value to your practice, helping you navigate the path to emotional strength and flexibility with expert support and insight.

If the journey to emotional resilience resonates with you and you're interested in exploring personalized guidance, we're here to support you. Our empowerment programs and emotional resilience training offerings are tailored to meet individual needs, providing you with the tools and insights needed to navigate life's challenges with grace and strength. To learn more about how we can assist you on this path, visit our website or feel free to send us an email. Your journey towards a more empowered self could start today.

Chapter 10

PHYSICAL MASTERY - THE TEMPLE OF STRENGTH

Physical health is more than a routine or obligation; it is a celebration of our natural state of being, a profound embodiment of your inner strength, your agility, and your grace. Our bodies, intricate and powerful, are designed to move, react, and engage with the world around us. They are the temples that house our soul and mirror our vigor, resilience, and competence. As individuals, it is our responsibility to cultivate physical abilities that transcend superficial aesthetics and reach into real-world applications.

These abilities allow us to protect and defend ourselves and those we care about, to overcome life's physical challenges, and to 'defeat our demons' both metaphorically and literally.

Whether it's rescuing a child from imminent danger, warding off a potential threat, or merely having the vitality to thrive in daily life, our physical health is a testament to our readiness and capability.

As parents, guardians, or role models, our strength, agility, and fortitude set a potent example, forging a legacy of empowerment and resilience that we pass on to the next generation. By honoring our bodies as sacred vessels, we affirm our commitment to nurturing, protecting, and mastering the physical aspect of our existence. It is not merely a means to an end but a vital component of a holistic, harmonious life, where body, mind, and spirit synergize in unison.

The Importance of Physical Health in Mastering Your Demons

The essence of physical health goes beyond mere fitness; it's about empowerment and self-realization. The capability to defend oneself, to support a loved one, or to overcome a life-threatening situation is the most primal and vital aspect of our existence. It aligns us with our ancient instincts of survival and nurtures our mental fortitude. Being physically fit isn't just about looking good; it's about being ready, capable, and indomitable.

Case Study: A Personal Journey to Physical Mastery

The Author's Experience

My pursuit of physical mastery began not as a mere hobby or aesthetic goal but as a profound quest for self-improvement, strength, empowerment, and self-protection. Engaging in a disciplined routine of weightlifting, cardio, martial arts, and self-awareness, I committed to forging my body as a temple of strength and resilience.

Facing the real threat of street violence, both armed and unarmed, my journey took on a deeper significance. The rigorous training sessions required to attain my level in Krav Maga martial arts were not just physical trials but lessons in fortitude, adaptability, and self-discovery. Every challenge became an opportunity to grow, to learn, and to redefine my limits.

This path led me to triumph over physical and mental obstacles, enabling me not only to defend myself in critical situations but to unlock a profound connection with my body, mind, and inner strength. The mastery I achieved was not confined to self-preservation; it became a tool to inspire and guide others in their pursuit of physical health and capability.

The satisfaction of knowing that my dedication has translated into the ability to protect myself, my loved ones, and to help thousands reach similar successes is immeasurable. It's more than a story; it's a living testament to the transformative power of discipline, dedication, and understanding the body as a sacred vessel.

Your body is your temple, and your strength is your legacy. This journey is an invitation to you, the reader, a motivational call to discover your own physical mastery, to nurture, protect, and honor the incredible gift that is your body. It's a path filled with potential, joy, and empowerment, waiting for you to embark upon.

Exercises for a healthy, able body

Embracing Responsibility: Your Body, Your Gift

Before embarking on the path to physical mastery, it's crucial to recognize and eliminate potential obstacles that might cause you to quit early or delay your journey towards a healthy body. While training with a friend can be motivating, it may also turn into more of a social hangout, diverting focus from your training session. More importantly, you must avoid becoming reliant on someone else's presence to engage in your training. Your body is your gift in life, and the responsibility for nurturing it rests solely with you.

As we have discussed in previous chapters, don't let inner demons like the comfort trap or fear of failure hinder your progress. Emphasize perseverance, discipline, and self-reliance to accomplish your physical goals. Remember, the path to physical mastery aligns closely with the mental and emotional strengths we've cultivated throughout this book.

The journey you're about to undertake is not just about building muscles or stamina; it's about strengthening the entirety of who you are, connecting with your inner self, and honoring your body as the sacred temple of strength it is.

1. **Cardio Program:** Engage in walking, running, swimming, cycling, or other cardio exercises for at least 30 minutes, three days a week, building up to daily practice. Consistency is key; schedule your sessions at the same time each day to build a habit, using discipline to overcome the comfort trap. Be flexible as an exception but stay committed.

2. **Weightlifting Routine:** Develop a balanced weightlifting program targeting different muscle groups three days a week. Emphasize form and mindfulness to connect with your body and build strength without overtraining. Don't rush; allow your body to grow and adapt gradually, in alignment with your overall wellness. There are many free weightlifting programs online to get started. Be responsible with the amount of weight and don't overtrain.

3. **Martial Arts Training:** Engage in modern combat martial arts training at least twice a week to enhance self-defense skills, discipline, and mindfulness. Connect with your inner warrior and employ emotional control from earlier chapters as you develop technique and awareness.

4. **Basic Body-Weight Routines:** If starting fresh, begin with daily sets of 50 push-ups, sit-ups, and squats. Break them down into a manageable 2 or 3 sets, employing discipline and routine to further lose weight and create muscle definition. Commit 3-4 days a week to form a lasting habit, using affirmations to keep you motivated.

5. **Diet and Rest:** Pay close attention to nourishment and recovery, aligning your diet and rest patterns with your physical needs. Treat your body with respect and kindness, nourishing it with balanced meals and ensuring adequate sleep. Reflect on your daily food intake to understand how it supports your physical mastery goals.

6. **Slow and Steady Approach:** Focus on long-term sustainability over quick transformations. Embrace patience, mindfulness, and understanding of your body to prevent injuries and build a strong foundation. Keep a journal of your progress, reflecting on how you feel and adapt over specific periods of time.

7. **Integrate Mind and Body:** Make your physical training a holistic practice by combining it with mindfulness techniques from previous chapters. Focus on your breathing, sensations, and mental clarity as you exercise, creating a synergistic connection between mind, body, and soul.

Physical mastery is indeed a lifelong commitment, reflecting not just our strength but our wisdom, understanding, and alignment with our inner potential. By integrating these exercises into your daily life, you embrace the sacred path toward self-realization, empowerment, and contentment, fully honoring the temple of strength within you.

Self-Mastery

VICTORY OVER YOUR DEMONS

Living a Life of Self-Mastery

Life is an ongoing journey filled with battles and triumphs. As we've explored in the preceding chapters, self-mastery is not merely a destination but an evolving process. It requires constant attention to self-awareness, discipline, emotional resilience, and physical health.

Self-Awareness: Your conquest over your demons began with introspection and awareness. Understanding the "comfort trap" and learning to escape instant gratification has set you on a path towards a life of long-term satisfaction and empowerment.

Discipline: Building and sustaining discipline through tangible activities like gym workouts, martial arts, and focused goal-setting has provided you the ultimate weapon against complacency and procrastination. This discipline has formed a foundation for achieving and maintaining success in other areas of life.

Emotional Resilience: The cultivation of emotional strength and flexibility has allowed you to harness the power of emotions like anger, sadness, and happiness. This has enabled you to connect deeply with yourself and others and act with wisdom and compassion.

Physical Mastery: Your physical body is the temple of strength. Through commitment to regular exercise and martial arts, you've built a physique capable of defending yourself and your loved ones, and a mental fortitude that transcends mere physicality.

The Path of Mastery Through Repetition:

In my years of practicing and teaching martial arts, I've discovered an essential truth about learning and mastery: repetition is key. Many actions require being practiced 25-50 times to become learned functions at the basic level, performed 100-150 times to be executed with ease, and repeated 350-1000 times to become second nature. With discipline and consistent practice, performing the same action between 5000-10000 times or more can lead to expertise or mastery.

The application of this numerical strategy can unlock our potential to learn and adapt to any new habit or skill, allowing us to understand the way we learn. For example, practicing a new skill only 10-25 times a day, 4 days a week for 1 month, can lead to 160-400 repetitions and the level of adeptness. Calculate how much time is required for one repetition and apply this strategy. Check the results after the set amount of time you've given yourself. This approach transcends limiting beliefs and judgments, empowering us to become experts in any area we desire.

Living a life of self-mastery means continued growth, evolution, and adaptation. It's a path towards enlightenment and true fulfillment, where every achievement fuels the next challenge.

Preparing for New Battles

Victory over your current demons does not mean the end of the battle. Life will always present new challenges and struggles. Here's how to prepare:

1. **Stay Committed**: Maintain your commitment to self-improvement, personal growth, and lifelong learning. Your journey doesn't end with a single triumph.

2. **Build on Successes**: Each victory gives you the confidence and skills to face the next battle. Reflect on what you've learned and apply these lessons to new challenges.

3. **Stay Mindful and Aware**: Continue to practice mindfulness, meditation, and introspection to stay connected with your inner self. Recognize new comfort traps and confront them with the tools you've honed.

4. **Physical and Mental Training**: Keep up with your physical exercises, mental practices, and emotional training.

Your body and mind need continuous nurturing to stay strong and resilient.

5. **Seek Support**: You don't have to face your battles alone. Seek out and lean on friends, family, mentors, or professionals who understand your journey and can provide guidance and encouragement.

6. **Celebrate Your Triumphs**: Acknowledge and celebrate your victories, no matter how small. They are milestones in your journey and deserve recognition.

In conclusion, victory over your demons is a continuous process of self-discovery, growth, and mastery. It's a fulfilling and enriching path that rewards those who dare to take it with inner strength, joy, and the profound satisfaction of living a life true to oneself.

Afterword

YOUR ONGOING JOURNEY

The chapters of this book have unfolded the path to triumph over your demons, but as you close these pages, remember that your journey is far from over. What has been laid out is not a finite course but a blueprint for continuous growth, exploration, and self-mastery.

Your ongoing journey is a personal one, unique to you. While the principles and exercises shared here provide guidance, your path will be shaped by your experiences, choices, and the wisdom you gain along the way.

Embrace Lifelong Learning: Never stop seeking knowledge and wisdom. Whether it's through books, mentors, or personal experiences, continue to expand your understanding of yourself and the world around you.

Stay Connected to Your Core Values: As you grow and evolve, your values will guide you. Revisit them regularly, ensure that your actions align with what truly matters to you, and be willing to adjust as needed.

Celebrate and Reflect: Take the time to celebrate your achievements and reflect on your struggles. Both are integral to your growth and offer valuable lessons.

Encourage Others: Share your journey with others. Your triumphs and lessons learned can be a source of inspiration and encouragement to those facing similar battles.

Keep Moving Forward: The road to self-mastery is a winding one, filled with unexpected turns and obstacles. Embrace them as opportunities for growth and keep moving forward with courage and conviction.

Create Your Legacy: Think about the legacy you want to leave behind. Your victories over your demons are not merely personal triumphs; they are part of the larger story of your life and the impact you have on others.

This book has been a glimpse into a profound and empowering process that has the potential to transform every aspect of your life. As you continue this path, know that you possess the inner strength, resilience, and wisdom to achieve true mastery over your demons.

May your ongoing journey be filled with discovery, fulfillment, and unending growth. Here's to your victory, today and always.

Appendix

FURTHER RESOURCES AND READING

As we conclude this exploration of self-discovery and empowerment, it is crucial to note that the journey doesn't end here. The themes, exercises, and philosophies that have been expounded in these chapters extend far beyond the confines of this book. For those eager to delve deeper into these subjects and continually progress on their path, the following resources are available:

Tools for Your Journey

1. **defeat-your-demons.com** - A haven for enthusiasts and warriors on their journey to victory, featuring a collection of motivational clothing and accessories branded with the Defeat Your Demons logo and artwork. Represent your triumph and inspire others on their path.

2. **ryansibelo.com** - Your go-to resource for tailored empowerment coaching packages, small group packages, and exclusive booking opportunities for signings, coaching, or speaking events. Make the most of this platform to connect, learn, and grow.

3. **Curzo.nl** - An avenue for self-defense and empowerment, offering Krav Maga classes for children and adults in the Netherlands. It also hosts business workshops, seminars, and workshops for civilians, providing ample opportunities to learn and master this empowering martial art.

4. **krav-maga.com** - The premier global platform for Krav Maga training, established by Master Eyal Yanilov. Harness the potential of this resource to develop your self-defense skills and elevate your physical and mental resilience.

These platforms serve as dynamic extensions of the principles and practices encapsulated in this book. They exist not only as repositories of information, but as thriving communities dedicated to the journey of self-mastery.

Engage with these resources, imbibe the wisdom they offer, and utilize them as companions on your unending voyage towards personal triumph.

Remember, the path to self-mastery is a lifelong journey - every step, every stumble, every victory is part of the process. Continue to learn, evolve, and ultimately, defeat your demons.

Acknowledgments

Embarking on this journey of self-discovery, empowerment, and mastery has been an incredible experience, one that would not have been possible without the support, guidance, and inspiration of countless remarkable individuals.

To all the amazing people I've met, trained with, or have been taught by, thank you for allowing me to grow and develop both as a person and in my field. Your dedication, wisdom, and camaraderie have shaped me in ways words can hardly express.

A heartfelt thank you to all the contributors for their awe-inspiring stories of strength, resilience, and growth. Your courage is a testament to the human spirit, and I am so proud to know you and be there with you on the journey to Defeat Your Demons.

A special acknowledgment goes to Master Eyal Yanilov from Krav Maga Global, the entire Global Instructor Team, all my colleague instructors, friends, and the KMG staff. Your teachings and developments in Krav Maga ignited my passion for martial arts, fueling my quest towards self-mastery. The lessons I've learned will forever resonate with me, and the friendships I've made over the years are treasures I hold dear. I'm proud to be part of the KMG community.

Lastly, I extend my heartfelt gratitude to my family, especially my children and wife, who have been my pillars of strength. To my 'chosen' family, your unwavering support and love have enriched my journey. To my readers, students, and everyone who has supported me throughout this fulfilling endeavor, your belief in me has been a source of endless encouragement. Together, you have all played an invaluable role in making this work possible, and I am eternally grateful.

May we all continue to grow, face our challenges with courage, and find victory in our pursuit of self-mastery.

I dedicate this book to Matthias, one of my dearest friends, business partners and "chosen" family. You left this world way too soon. But your memory, spirit and our friendship will be forever etched in my heart.

Thank you, dear reader, for embarking on this journey with me. Your dedication to self-improvement and the pursuit of mastery is a testament to the strength and potential within us all. May the lessons and insights you've discovered in these pages guide you towards a life of empowerment and fulfillment. Here's to our shared path toward conquering our inner demons and triumphing in life.

About the Author

Ryan Sibelo, born in the Netherlands and raised in Zoetermeer and Dallas, Georgia, USA, has over the years very actively been engaged in the lifelong pursuit of mastery, empowerment, and victory over his inner demons. A childhood fascination with martial arts and the hero archetype set him on a path filled with both trials and triumphs. Ryan recognizes that the journey to transcend inner demons is an ongoing process, one that requires constant self-awareness, growth, and dedication, and he invites others to join him in this never-ending quest for self-mastery.

Ryan's early life was marked by family challenges, insecurities, and a constant search for validation. These struggles led him on a path of introspection, where he sought to understand the roots of his behavior and the ways in which he could overcome them. Through self-awareness, he began to discern why he behaved in certain ways and where those patterns stemmed from. Embracing the disciplines of martial arts, he found empowerment, not only physically but mentally, by applying the principles of hard work, consistency, and dedication. These achievements gradually nurtured a belief in himself, transforming his struggles into strengths and setting the foundation for his lifelong quest for self-mastery.

Intent on overcoming these personal hurdles, he delved into various martial arts, ultimately finding his calling in Krav Maga. Under the tutelage of Master Eyal Yanilov, he achieved an Expert 2 level, transforming not only his physical abilities but his entire mindset. His passion for self-improvement went beyond the dojo. He engaged in different seminars and courses to develop a holistic approach to empowerment, embodying principles now central to this book.

Ryan is the owner of Curzo and Defeat Your Demons brand. He is a Krav Maga Global Expert and Combat & Fighting instructor, also coaching resilience, team building, and violence prevention in the workplace. As an empowerment trainer and non-verbal communication expert, he offers conversation techniques for de-escalation and conflict resolution. His achievements in both personal and professional realms are a testament to his dedication, discipline, and passion.

Outside his professional life, Ryan enjoys spending time with friends and family, traveling, enjoying music, cooking, engaging in various sports, and indulging in his enthusiasm for technology.

Ryan's mission with this book is to empower readers to face their challenges, connect with their inner strength, and achieve triumph in life. Through his personal experiences and teachings, he offers practical strategies and insights that can be applied to daily life. This guidance is not limited to the pages of this book but extends to a wealth of resources and personalized support available online.

For those seeking further inspiration, coaching, empowerment packages, or simply a way to connect with the Defeat Your Demons community, explore the following platforms:

- defeat-your-demons.com, for motivational clothing and accessories

- ryansibelo.com, for personal and small group empowerment or Krav Maga coaching

- curzo.nl , for Krav Maga classes and business workshops in the Netherlands

- krav-maga.com, the worldwide source for Krav Maga training by Master Eyal Yanilov

Ryan's wish is that readers find value in this book and share its message, becoming allies in the collective journey towards self-mastery.